section

ral heritage and
abitats, annotated
ecialist authors and

The impact of
tional events on
e earliest days to
tion at a glance
aring in a timeline
uscan language in
form.

Typical Tuscan
es and their
ontemporary life.
hitectural heritage:
d urban dwellings
oments in civil,
us architecture with
le and typology.
A selection of works
14th century to the
ting an informative
art.
n anthology of texts
f all periods and
thematically.

itineraries begins
area to be explored.
These sites,
boxes, should be

sites (also in gray
by the editor for
wing to their key
eptional beauty.
ated double-page
tlight on subjects
-depth treatment.

nformation

rmation you will need
when you get there.
andy table listing the
ening hours of all the
red in this guide.
A selection of hotels
mpiled by a specialist.
raphy, list of
of names and index
ces.
iled maps of all the
the guide, followed
index and a map of
nce.

◆ NORTHERN TUSCANY

◆ NORTHERN TUSCA

Each map in
this section is
designated by a
letter while the
letters and figures
of the grid
references make it
easy for the reader
to pinpoint sites
featured in this
guide (for example
B C3).

D0724030

CHIANTI ▲ 202

SIENA ▲ 208

SAN GIMIGNANO ▲ 225

PIENZA ▲ 232

VOLTERRA ▲ 236

TUSCAN ARCHIPELAGO ▲ 244

ntinues to enjoy an
international reputation.

PISA
Renowned for its
spectacular 'Square of
Miracles', one of the
finest expressions of
municipal pride, this
dynamic university town
has much to offer.

LUCCA
An exquisite, secluded
city, still protected by its
intact ring of walls.

AREZZO
This inland Tuscan city
boasts an array of
treasures, including one
of the most beautiful
squares in Italy and the
fresco cycle of the *Legend
of the True Cross*.

SANSEPOLCRO
The city of Piero della
Francesca contains various
masterpieces by one of
the leading exponents of
Renaissance art.

CORTONA
Etruscan walls, cobbled
lanes, medieval houses
and Renaissance and
baroque palaces combine
to create an unusually
harmonious whole.

CHIANTI
If there is a heaven for
wine, it is Chianti: a small
region between Florence
and Siena, whose
landscape is dominated
by grapevines.

SIENA
An extensive artistic
heritage and a renewed
sense of purpose. Siena
is living proof that the
Middle Ages can survive
into the third millennium.

SAN GIMIGNANO
Walls and towers
guarding the Via
Francigena: this city is
regarded as the epitome
of a medieval city.

PIENZA
The Renaissance dream of
Pope Pius II, realized by
architect Rossellino.

VOLTERRA
One of the best preserved
free towns in Italy
surrounded by the
spectacular dramatic
landscape of the balze.

TUSCAN ARCHIPELAGO
A string of seven islands
predominantly covered by
dense Mediterranean
vegetation in the largest
protected marina area in
the Mediterranean.

TUSCA

The mini-map locates the itinerary within the wider area covered by the guide.

The itinerary map outlines the route to be taken and shows the main sites and places of special interest.

◆ **C** D4
This reference enables you to locate the site on one of the maps in the map section.

1. Arezzo ▲ 184
2. Sansepolcro ▲ 190
3. La Verna, the Casentino and the Hermitages ▲ 194
4. Toward the 'New Town' ▲ 197
5. The Valdichiana ▲ 198
6. Cortona ▲ 199

THE JOUST OF THE SARACEN
Twice a year, in June and September, the Joust of the Saracen takes place in the Piazza Grande. This ancient tournament first took place in the Renaissance.

FAMOUS PEOPLE FROM AREZZO
The many artists who have secured Arezzo's fame include Guittone d'Arezzo (c. 1230–94), Pietro Aretino (1492–1556), Francesco Petrarch (1304–74) and Giorgio Vasari (1511–74) (below, Vasari's bust in Corso Italia in Arezzo). Vasari was a dominant figure: architect and historiographer, he made his mark on history as did his pupil Pietro Aretino, a hard-hitting writer.

Arezzo is fascinating both as a hill town and as a rich storehouse of well-preserved works of art. Despite the fact that urban expansion has created some extensive commercial zones, visitors to the city can still catch a tantalizing whiff of the countryside. The bastions continue to be surrounded by vineyards and besieged by olive trees, while the city's glorious works of art radiate such a glow that they seem to light the visitor's way. It is hardly surprising that Piero della Francesca ▲ 192 became the idol of many 20th-century painters. The territory of Arezzo boasts many unique architectural gems including great Franciscan and Camaldolese sanctuaries, Etruscan strongholds such as Cortona and ideal Renaissance cities such as dazzling Sansepolcro. Arezzo is unique among the hill towns in central Italy: the city was built on the south-facing slope of a modest hill, which means that every part of the city receives an equal dappling of light and shadow. Situated at the convergence of four valleys steeped in history – the upper Arno valley, the Casentino, the Valdichiana and the Valtiberina – Arezzo has always been a meeting point and a trade forum. This strategic position meant that anyone wanting to control this region had to control this city, which is why Florence has exerted its dominion over Arezzo since 1384.

184

AREZZO: THREE PHASES OF HISTORY ◆ C D4

The history of the city can be divided into three periods: the Etruscan period, when *Aretium* sprang up on the hill delimited by what are today the church, the fortress and the Duomo; the Roman period, when the hill town became an important military center on the Via Cassia; and its time as a *comune*, which began in 1008 with the first consuls and ended in 1384 when Arezzo was finally conquered by Florence.

THE ARTISTIC HEART OF THE CITY

SAN FRANCESCO. Visitors to Arezzo generally start their tour of the city in the Piazza San Francesco, which is at the center of the oldest part of the city. Here stands the church of San Francesco, which is the custodian, among other things, of the masterpiece by Piero della Francesca, the *Legend of the True Cross* (*detail, below*). This church is a 13th-century Gothic structure rebuilt between 1318 and 1377 and restored in the early 20th century. Its 15th-century campanile towers over a stone and brick façade that was never completed (parts of the facing designed in the 14th century are kept in the basement). In the choir of the church of San Francesco visitors can admire the frescos

A CITY SHAPED LIKE A SHIP ✪
As early as the Middle Ages it was noticed that Arezzo's walls formed the shape of a ship, with its prow pointing toward Florence. This ship is laden with treasures, ranging from the paintings of Piero della Francesco to the symmetrical Piazza Grande, one of the finest and most original squares in Italy. There are also monuments of medieval religious architecture and cultural events like the antiques fair and the Joust of the Saracen.

THE PALAZZO DEL GOVERNO
In the western part of the city, at Poggio del Sole, stands the Palazzo del Governo built by Giovanni Michelucci in 1938–40. The building is very interesting because it makes reference to the most important monuments in Arezzo's architectural tradition, from its concave appearance reminiscent of the Convento degli Olivetani and the Logge Vasariane, to the architraved portico that makes reference to the façade of the Church of Santa Maria. The statues on the covered roof-terrace represent a nod to the Palazzo Arbergotti. A fine example of modernism, this building resembles a metaphorical architectural patternbook.

In front, the gate of San Lorentino; in the background, the massive structure of the Duomo towers above the densely packed medieval city.

185

★ The star denotes sites, events and monuments singled out by the editor for special attention.

● ▲ ◆ The symbols within the text provide cross-references to a site discussed elsewhere in the guide.

✪ This symbol indicates places that should not be missed.

● Encyclopedia section

▲ <u>Itineraries in Tuscany</u>

◆ <u>Practical information</u>

FLORENCE ▲ 115
One of the most frequently visited cities of art in the world: a showcase of Medieval and Renaissance art and architecture.

CHIANTI ▲ 201
Castles, hamlets, villas and farmhouses in the land of wine and olive oil: a landscape that has been three thousand years in the making.

AROUND FLORENCE ▲ 139. Explore the Arno Valley, home of Leonardo da Vinci, and the Val di Pesa, dotted with Medici villas, hamlets and monasteries.

SIENA ▲ 207
The home of the Campo, the Palio, Simone Martini and Saint Catherine: this is one of the most symbolic cities of the Italian civilization.

PISA AND LUCCA ▲ 145. Two great cities with a glorious past divided for centuries by a bitter hatred and united by a magnificent Romanesque culture.

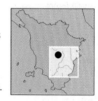

AROUND SIENA ▲ 223. Manmade landscapes, art treasures and the natural beauty of the hills from the Val d'Elsa to Mount Amiata.

MASSA, CARRARA AND THE APUAN ALPS ▲ 163. A long narrow strip of land lying between the Apuan Alps, scored by the white scars of marble quarries, and the Tyrrhenian coast.

FROM VOLTERRA TO LIVORNO ▲ 235
Unspoiled nature and sophisticated architecture; the ancient Via Aurelia along the coast; the Tuscan Archipelago.

PRATO AND PISTOIA ▲ 173
Two cities now almost suburbs of Florence, but proud of their own distinctive cultural identity.

GROSSETO AND THE MAREMMA ▲ 252
From the geometric landscape of the reclaimed coastal plain to the inland plateaus.

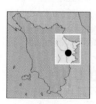

AREZZO AND ITS SURROUNDINGS ▲ 183. A region endowed with numerous religious buildings and one of the cradles of the Renaissance.